For inquiries, licensing, or bulk orders, contact:
connect2reeharris@gmail.com

ISBN (eBook): 979-8-9997683-0-8
ISBN (Paperback): 979-8-9997683-1-5

This publication is intended for educational and informational purposes only. While every effort has been made to ensure the accuracy of the content, neither the author nor the publisher assumes responsibility for any actions or outcomes based on the information provided. Readers should always conduct independent research and consult professionals when necessary.

Cover design and interior layout by Ree Harris
First Edition – 2025
Printed in the United States of America

CONTENTS

INTRODUCTION

Welcome to Content-to-Cash on Autopilot!

If you're ready to start earning money passively—with no need for a large social media following or a complicated tech setup—you're in the right place.

This guide is designed for beginners who want to tap into the power of AI tools like Chat GPT to build simple, scalable income streams.

You'll learn:

- How to generate and sell eBooks, workbooks, templates, and more
- How to use AI prompts to eliminate guesswork and writer's block
- How to start monetizing—even if you have no audience right now
- How to automate your digit al product business as much as possible

By the end, you'll be able to create your first (or next) product in hours and start selling it with simple systems.

Let's dive in!

WHAT IS CHAT GPT

Chat GPT is a free (or low-cost) AI tool that can: · Write, edit, and brainstorm content · Create business ideas and outlines · Help you publish digital pr oducts · Build marketing copy and email sequences The best part? You don't need to be tech-savvy. You just need to know how to prompt it effectively—and this guide gives you the exact prompts to use.

KEY PASSIVE INCOME IDEAS

You can use Chat GPT to help you create and sell:

- Digital eBooks (guides, how-to manuals, knowledge summaries)
- Low-content books (journals, planners, trackers)
- Printable templates (checklists, habit trackers, planners)
- Online courses (AI can draft outlines and video scripts)
- Digital prompts packs (for writers, content creators, coaches)
- Newsletter conten t (to later monetize with ads or sponsors)

Each of these can be made once a nd sold forever.

WRITING/FORMATTING

Using AI tooutline, write,andformatnonfiction ebooks or low-content books (like journals, planners, work books).

Include specific and detailed AI prompts and try to give your audience real value they can use immediately.

Prompt for Non-Fiction eBook:
"Act as a best-selling non-fiction author. Create a detailed outline for a [topic] ebook for [target audience]. Include chapters and bullet points for each section."

- Example:
"Act as a best-selling non-fiction author. Create a detailed outline for a 'Confidence for Creators' ebook targeting beginner entrepreneurs. Include 8 chapters with key points under each."

Prompt for Workbook or Journal:
"Create a structured outline for a [number of days/weeks] [journal/planner/workbo ok] on [topic]. Include sections like prompts, reflections, exercises, or habit trackers."

- Example:
"Create a structured outline for a 30-day self-love journal for women. Include daily prompts, affirmation spaces, and weekly reflection pages."

Prompt to Write Chapter Content (Non-Fiction):

"Write a first draft for Chapter [X] of a book on [topic] for [audience]. The chapter should cover: [insert 3–5 bullet points]. Use a friendly, motivational tone."

- Example:

"Write Chapter 3 of a book about overcoming fear for new entrepreneurs. Cover: (1) how fear blocks creativity, (2) common fears for content creators, (3) mindset reframes, (4) action tips."

Prompt for Journal Pages:

"Create 30 unique daily journal prompts for a [topic] journal. Keep them reflective, thought-provoking, and short enough for one paragraph answers."

- Example:

"Create 30 unique prompts for a gratitude journal for stressed-out moms. Keep them warm, simple, and emotionally grounding."

Prompt for Planner Layout:

"Design a weekly planner layout for [goal] including sections like goals, priorities, task list, schedule, and motivational quotes."

- Example:

"Design a weekly planner layout for content creators. Include sections for content ideas, post schedule, daily task tracker, and engagement log."

STEP 3: ENHANCE THE CONTENT WITH STRUCTURE AND FORMATTING

Prompt for Formatting Suggestions:
"How should I format this book in Google Docs or Canva for print-on-demand? Include font sizes, margin tips, and layout for paperback."

- Example:
"I'm formatting a 100-page daily productivity planner in Canva for KDP. What font sizes, page margins, and layout tips do you recommend for a 6x9" paperback?"

Prompt to Add Headings, Call-outs, & Lists:
"Revise this chapter to include bold section headings, numbered lists where needed, and short call-out boxes with key takeaways."

- Example:
"Revise this chapter on time blocking to include a bold heading for each concept, 1 numbered list, and 2 boxes with actionable tips."

STEP 4: RE-PURPOSE OR EXPA ND YOUR BOOK (OPTIONAL)

Prompt to Create a Companion Workbook:
"Turn this e-book on [topic] into a companion workbook with exercises, journal prompts, and checklist pages."

- Example:
"Turn my e-book on 'Marketing for Coaches' into a workbook with weekly exercises, journal prompts, and a 30-day content checklist."

Prompt to Create a Bundle:

"Based on this [ebook/workbook], create 3 printable add-ons I can sell as a bonus or bundle. Each should be practical and visually simple."

- Example:

"Create 3 add-on printables for my self-care planner: (1) affirmation cards, (2) weekly mood tracker, (3) 15-minute stress reset checklist."

BONUS PROMPT: USE THIS PROMPT TO BRAINSTORM ANY BOOK FAST

"Act as a digital product expert. Brainstorm 10 unique [ebook/journal/workbook] ideas for [niche or audience]. Focus on profitable and evergreen topics."

- Example:

"Act as a digital product expert. Brainstorm 10 workbook ideas for busy moms who want more balance and productivity."

PRINTABLES OR TEMPLETS

IDEA 1. CHECKLISTS

Checklists are popular because they're clear, actionable, and easy to use. You can profit more by bundling them with journals, planners, or e-books.

Prompt to create a daily routine checklist:
"Create a daily morning routine checklist for busy moms who want to start their day with peace and productivity. Include 8–10 steps with short, motivating language."

Prompt to create a business launch checklist:
"Design a 10-step business startup checklist for beginner entrepreneurs. Include practical steps from idea to first sale, using clear action language."

Prompt to format a checklist for printables:
Take this list of 10 tasks and reformat it as a printable checklist. Add short headers, bullet points, and blank check boxes next to each item."

Prompt to create a self-care checklist bundle:
"Create 3 themed self-care checklists: (1) Mental health, (2) Body wellness, and (3) End-of-day wind-down. Each should have 8 items and a soft, encouraging tone."

IDEA 2. AFFIRMATION CARDS

Affirmation cards are powerful, evergreen, and great for passive income. You can sell them as digital downloads or print-on-demand cards.

Prompt to create af firmations for women:

"Write 30 empowering affirmations for [your target audience]. Keep them short (1–2 lines), positive, and future-focused."

Prompt to create cards by category:

"Give me 5 affirmations each for the following categories: (1) Abundance, (2) Confidence, (3) Calmness, and (4) Creativity. Keep each affirmation under 10 words." (choose categories of your choice)

Prompt to create printable card text:

"Format these affirmations as if they were printed on 3x3 cards. Include a title, affirmation, and short closing reminder or mantra."

Prompt to add design notes for Canva:

"Suggest a minimalist Canva design for affirmation cards. Include recommended font styles, background colors, and where to place the text on each card."

IDEA 3. BUSINESS TEMPLATES

Business templates are great for coaches, service providers, and entrepreneurs. You can create them for emails, branding, planning, or clie nt workflows.

Prompt to create a lead magnet template:

"Create a 1-page lead magnet template for new coaches. Include sections for: Title, Problem Overview, Quick Tips, and Call-to-Action."

Prompt to create a social media content calendar:
"Design a 30-day Instagram content calendar for personal brands. Include themes for each day, caption ideas, and call to action suggestions."

Prompt to create a client on-boarding form:
"Create a simple client intake form template for a freelance graphic designer. Include questions about goals, style preferences, budget, and deadline."

Prompt to create a business expense tracker template:
"Design a business expense tracker layout for solopreneurs. Include columns for date, description, category, payment method, and total."

Prompt to turn this into a printable or Google Sheet:
"How can I format this business expense tracker for Canva as a printable PDF and for Google Sheets as a fillable spreadsheet?'

NOTE: USE AI + CANVA TOGETHER

Once ChatGPT gives you the structure and wording, copy that text into Canva, choose a template or blank page, and format it w ith:

- Custom fonts & colors

- Icons, checkboxes, or divider lines

Export as PDF for printables or PNG for cards

PUBLISH AND EARN

Publish online and earn passive income every time someone buys.

STEP 1: FORMAT FOR PUBLISHING

Prompt to get KDP specs:

"I'm publishing a [number of pages in book] paperback journal on Amazon KDP. What bleed settings, margin sizes, and file formats do I need for the interior and cover?"

Prompt to get Canva cover design help:

"Suggest a Canva layout for a minimalist affirmation journal cover or [your product]. Recommend font styles, colors, and where to place the title, subtitle, and author name."

STEP 2: UPLOAD & SET UP FOR SALE

Prompt to walk through uploading:

"Walk me through the ste ps to upload, price, and automate delivery for [your product] on [online store of your choice]. I want to sell a downloadable PDF."

Prompt to generate a product listing description:

"Write a product description for a 30-day gratitude journal digital download or [your product]. Use clear, friendly language and include keywords like 'self-care', 'mental wellness', and 'journal prompts'."

Prompt to write a short store bio: "Write a 2–3 sentence bio for my online store that sells self-development digital planners, journals, and printables." Or [your product]

STEP 3: PROMOTE & AUTOMATE

Prompt to create a 5-day launch content plan:
"Create a 5-day launch plan to promote a new passive income e-book. Include one post idea and call-to-action per day."

Prompt to write a promotional caption:
"Write an Instagram caption for launching a productivity planner. Keep it motivational and include a call-to-action to click the bio link."

Prompt to automate delivery emails:
"How do I set up automatic delivery and thank-you emails for digital product buyers?"

BONUS: IMPROVE, UP-SELL, AND SCALE

Prompt to analyze and improve a product listing:
"Here's my current listing for a 30-day self-care journal: [paste your listing]. Ho w can I improve this to get more sales?"

Prompt to create bundle/up-sell ideas:
"Based on my digital planner for entrepreneurs, give me 3 simple bonus products I could include in a bundle to increase sales."

EARN PASSIVE INCOME ONLINE

Selling digital products online is one of the easiest and most profitable ways to earn passive income. Whether it's a journal, planner, template, or e-book, once you set up your system, the sales can roll in with little effort. Here's how to automate the process using AI.

STEP 1: CHOOSE THE RIGHT PLATFORM TO SELL

You can sell your digital products on various platforms like Gumroad, Etsy, Payhip, or Amazon KDP. Each has its unique strengths, so choose which one is best for your product.

Prompt to compare selling platforms:
"What are the pros and cons of selling digital products on Gumroad, Etsy, Amazon KDP, and Payhip? Which platform is best for [your product] for beginners?"

BONUS: PLATFORM COMPARISON. CHAT GPT WILL BE MORE DETAILED

- Gumroad: Great for simple digital downloads and instant payouts, but less exposure.

- Etsy: Ideal for printables with an audience already browsing for them, but requires SEO work.

- Amazon KDP: Huge reach with Kindle and paperback options, but royalties are lower.

- Payhip: Simple platform with great features for recurring payments but smaller reach.

STEP 2: SET UP YOUR STOREFRONT

Setting up a storefront is easy on platforms like Etsy and Gumroad. You want to convert visitors into customers with a professional yet inviting layout. You can also use other platforms listed in this book.

Prompt to set up Gumroad store:

"How do I set up a professional storefront on Gumroad or [your preferred platform] to sell [your product]? Walk me through uploading my digital files, setting up pricing, and automating delivery."

Prompt to set up Etsy shop for digital downloads:

"Give me step-by-step instructions to set up my Etsy store or [your preferred store] for selling products like [your product]. Include tips on pricing, SEO, and product tags."

STEP 3: CREATE A SALES PAGE FOR YOUR PRODUCT

The sales page is where your potential customers will decide to buy or leave. It's esse ntial to include all the right elements to convert visitors into buyers.

Prompt to wr ite a product description:

"Write a compelling product description for a 30-day gratitude journal or for [your product] that I'm selling. Use persuasive, customer-focused language and include keywords like 'digital download', 'gratitude', and 'self-care journal'."

Prompt to create a product listing

"Write a short and engaging product description for a self-care planner [or for your product]. Focus on how it helps people prioritize themselves and stay organized. Include a call to action to 'download now'."

STEP 4: SET UP PAYMENT & DELIVERY AUTOMATION

For a fully passive process, you need to automate payments and product delivery.

Prompt for payment setup:

"How can I set up automatic payments and delivery for my products on [the platform you chose]? Make sure I understand how to enable instant download for customers."

STEP 5: DRIVE TRAFFIC TO YOUR PRODUCTS (MARKETING)

Marketing is essential to drive visitors to your products. With Chat GPT, you can generate social media posts, email templates, and ads that automates most of the work.

Prompt to generate a social media content plan:

"Create a 5-day Instagram or [platform of your choice] content plan for launching [your product] or a new self-care journal. Include one post idea per day with a call to action, hashtags, and a link to my store."

Prompt to write a promotional email:

"Write a promotional email to my email list announcing my new product. [attach a photo of your product to the prompt for better accuracy]. Keep it friendly, use a compelling subject line, and include a discount code."

Prompt to create Ads copy:
"Write a Facebook ad copy [or any ad of your choice) for a digital planner [or your project] aimed at [your target audience]. Make it catchy and include a strong call to action to download now."

STEP 6: AUTOMATE CUSTOMER SUPPORT AND COMMUNICATION

You will need to automate customer support and follow-ups to keep everything running smoothly once customers start buying.

Prompt for automated thank-you email after purchase:
"Write a thank-you email template to send automatically after a purchase. Include a link to the product, instructions on how to download it, and a personal note of gratitude."

Prompt for a customer service email response template:
"Write a customer service email template that I can use to respond to questions about digital downloads. Make it polite, clear, and helpful."

STEP 7: OPTIMIZE & SCALE YOUR SALES

Once your store is set up and your sales are flowing, it's time to optimize and scale.

Prompt for product improvement:
"Review this product description for [your product] on my online store. How can I improve it to increase conversions?" (Paste your product description)

Prompt for creating bundles or up-sells:
"Suggest 3 product bundles or up-sell ideas for [your product] or for digital planners. How can I package them together to increase my revenue per customer?"

Once your store is running, you'll want to track sales and performance. Chat GPT can assist by generating tracking templates.

Prompt for sales tracking template in Google Sheets:
"Create a Google Sheets sales tracker template for digital product sales on [you preferred sales platform]. Include columns for date, product name, sales, revenue, and customer email."

Prompt for sales analysis report:
"How can I analyze sales data from [your sales platform] to identify trends and optimize my marketing strategies for product sales?"

LAUNCH A YOUTUBE OR TIKTOK CHANNEL

UsingAItogenerate scripts, captions, thumbnails , and video ideas

Content creation can feel overwhelming when beginning a YouTube channel or TikTok account. AI will handle much of the work for you from coming up with video ideas to writing scripts, creating captions, and even suggesting thumbnails. Use these prompts to automate your content creation process with Chat GPT.

STEP 1: GENERATE VIDEO IDEAS

The first step in launching a channel is figuring out what content to make. Use AI to help you brainstorm a large list of relevant and trending ideas.

Prompt to generate video ideas for YouTube or TikTok:

"Generate 10 viral video ideas for a YouTube channel about [topic]. Focus on providing value to [target audience]. Include topics that are trending in [year]."

- Example:

"Generate 10 viral video ideas for a YouTube channel about personal finance for beginners. Focus on providing tips for young adults starting to save and invest."

Prompt to get ideas for TikTok videos:

"Generate 10 short-form TikTok video ideas for a [niche]. Include hooks that grab attention and make people want to watch till the end."

- Example:

"Generate 10 short-form TikTok video ideas for a fitness coach. Focus on beginner-friendly workout routines and motivational tips."

STEP 2: WRITE SCRIPTS FOR VIDEOS

AI can write your script once you have your video ideas. From introductions to calls-to-actions.

Prompt to write a YouTube video script:

"Write a 5-minute YouTube script for [your video idea or topic]. Include an engaging intro, key tips, and a strong call-to-action."

- Example:

"Write a 5-minute YouTube script for a video on 'How to Start Budgeting as a College Student'. Include an engaging intro, key budgeting tips (e.g. savings, expenses), and encourage viewers to download my budgeting template."

Prompt to write a TikTok video script:

"Write a 60-second TikTok script for a video about [your topic]. Include a catchy hook, value-packed tips, and an engaging CTA at the end."

- Example:

"Write a 60-second TikTok script on '3 Easy Ways to Start a business 20s'. Start with a hook, provide tips, and ask viewers to email me for more information." (add the customers email to an automated email list)

STEP 3: CREATE VIDEO CAPTIONS

Captions are key to driving engagement for YouTube and TikTok videos. AI can help write catchy, SEO-friendly captions that encourage viewers to like, share, and comment.

Prompt to write YouTube video captions:
"Write a YouTube video description for a video on 'How to Create a Passive Income Stream in 2025'. Use relevant keywords like 'passive income', 'financial freedom', and 'online business'."

- Example:
"Write a YouTube video description for a video on 'How to Create a Passive Income Stream in 2025'. Include keywords like 'passive income', 'financial freedom', 'money-making ideas', and encourage viewers to subscribe for more tips."

Prompt to write TikTok captions:
"Write an engaging TikTok caption for a video on [your topic]. Include popular hashtags and a CTA to follow for more tips."

- Example:
"Write an engaging TikTok caption for a video on 'How to Set Realistic Fitness G oals in 2025'. Include hashtags like #fitnessgoals #newyearnewme and ask viewers to comment on their fitness goals for the year."

STEP 4: DESIGN THUMBNAILS

Thumbnails are key for getting people to click on your YouTube videos, and AI can help suggest design elements and text for thumbnails.

Prompt to get thumbnail ideas for YouTube video:
"What should the thumbnail look like for a video on [your topic]? Suggest image ideas and text to include."

- Example:

"What should the thumbna il look like for a video on 'How to Make Money Online in 2025'? Suggest a bold background color, include text like 'generational wealth in 2025', and include an image of a laptop and dollar signs."

Prompt to get thumbnail design ideas for TikTok video:
"Suggest thumbnail ideas for a TikTok video on [your topic]. Include text, color suggestions, and image ideas."

- Example:

"Suggest thumbnail ideas for a TikTok video on '5 Quick Home Workouts for Busy People'. Use bright, energetic colors like yellow and red, with bold text 'Quick Workouts', and an image of someone exercising at home."

STEP 5: OPTIMIZE YOUR CONTENT FOR ENGAGEMENT

AI can help you optimize your videos for a better chance to reach by suggesting engaging titles, tags, and hashtags.

Prompt to ge nerate YouTube video tags:
"Generate 10 SEO-friendly tags for a YouTube video on [your topic]. Use popular keywords for this topic."

- Example:

"Generate 10 SEO-friendly tags for a YouTube video on 'How to Build a Personal Brand in 2025'. Include 'personal branding', 'building a brand', 'social media marketing', and 'content creation'."

Prompt to generate TikTok hashtags:
"Generate 10 relevant TikTok hashtags for a video on [your topic]. Focus on trends and productivity."

- Example:

"Generate 10 relevant TikTok hashtags for a video on 'Simple Diet Hacks for Busy Professionals.' for Busy Professionals'. Focus on trends and productivity.

AUTOMATION: AUTOMATE YOUR CONTENT CREATION WORKFLOW

Now that you've learned how to use AI to generate video ideas, scripts, captions, and thumbnails, you can easily batch-create content for a whole week or month. This allows you to consistently upload fresh content on YouTube, TikTok, and other social platforms without having to start from scratch every time.

EDIT OR VOICE OVER, THEN MONETIZE WITH ADS

STEP 1: EDITING YOUR CONTENT

Editing videos, blogs, or social media content is very time-consuming. AI tools can help you save time significantly while maintaining high-quality content.

Prompt for improving written content (e.g., blog or e-book):

"Edit the following blog post for clarity, grammar, and SEO optimization. Keep the tone friendly and professional. Include keyword suggestions based on this text." (insert your post)

- Example:

"Edit the following blog post on 'How to Create Passive Income in 2025' for clarity, grammar, and SEO optimization. Focus on keywords like 'passive income', 'financial freedom', and 'side hu stle'."

Prompt for improving video script (e.g., YouTube or TikTok):

"Edit this video script for a YouTube video for readability, engagement, and clarity. Sugge st engaging hooks and transitions for each section."

- Example:

"Edit this video script for a YouTube video on 'How to Save Money in 2025'. Include hooks, engaging questions for viewers, and smooth transitions between sections."

Prompt for video content editing (using an AI video editor):

"How can I use AI tools like Descript or Runway to edit my video, remove filler words, and create jump cuts that improve viewer engagement? Provide step-by-step instructions."

- Example:

"How can I use AI tools like Descript or Runway to edit my video on 'Tips for Effective Budgeting'? Guide me through removing filler words, adding captions, and creating seamless transitions."

STEP 2: ADDING VOICE OVERS

The best thing for YouTube videos, podcasts, TikTok clips, and more is AI-generated voice overs . With tools like Descript or Murf.ai, you can easily create professional voice overs without needing to record them yourself.

Prompt to generate voice over for a video script:

"Generate a professional-sounding AI voice over for the following script [your script]. Make the voice warm, clear, and trustworthy."

- Example:

"Generate a professional-sounding AI voice over for this script on 'The Importan ce of Saving for Retirement'. Make it warm, clear, and trustworthy with a tone suitable for financial advice."

Prompt to generate an AI voice over with different tones:

"Generate three versions of this voice over with the following tones: (1)Friendly, (2)Authoritative, (3)Motivational. Each version should sound natural and engaging for a video on 'Building Financial Confidence'."

- Example:

"Generate three versions of this voiceover with different tones for the script on 'Building Financial Confidence': (1) Friendly, (2) Authoritative, (3) Motivational. Keep the voice energetic and positive."

Prompt to sync v oice over with video:

"How can I sync the AI voice over with my video in tools like Descript or Adobe Premiere Pro? Please provide detailed instructions on how to align audio and video for a smooth presentation."

- Example:

"How do I sync the AI voice over with my video on 'Money-Saving Tips' in Adobe Premiere Pro? Provide step-by-step instructions to align the voice over with video and make it sound natural."

STEP 3: MONETIZE WITH ADS AND AFFILIATE LINKS

Once your content is edited and ready, the next step is monetizing it with ads and affiliate marketing. AI tools can also help with finding the best affiliate programs and integrating ads into your content.

Prompt for setting up YouTube ads for monetization:

"How can I enable You Tube monetization and set up ads for my video on [your video topic]. Provide a step-by-step guide for YouTube ads, including ad types and targeting options."

- Example:

Guide me through setting up YouTube monetization and ad targeting for my video on 'How to Make Money Online in 2025'. What types of ads should I use to reach my target audience?"

Prompt to find affiliate programs for your niche:
"Search for affiliate programs in the [niche] space (e.g., finance, health, business). Recommend the best programs for beginners to promote on YouTube or TikTok videos."

- Example:
"Find affiliate programs in the personal finance niche. Recommend programs for beginners to promote on my YouTube channel about 'Building Passive Income'."

Prompt to add affiliate links to video descriptions:
"Write a YouTube video description with affiliate links for a video on [your video topic]. Include a CTA to check out the tools and affiliate links to the products."

- Example:
"Write a YouTube description for my video on 'Best Budgeting Tools for 2025'. Include a CTA to visit the link for the tools, with affiliate links to recommended products like 'Mint' and 'YNAB'."

STEP 4: TRACK PERFORMANCE & OPTIMIZE FOR MORE REVENUE

Once you start monetizing, track the performance of your content and ads to en sure maximum profitability. AI can also help you analyze data and optimize for better engagement.

Prompt to track ad revenue performance:
"How can I track the performance of my YouTube ads and ad revenue? What are the best metrics to measure, and how do I adjust my ad strategy to maximize revenue?"

- Example:
"How can I track YouTube ad revenue performance? Guide me through understanding the metrics like CPM, CPC, and CTR, and how to adjust my targeting for better results."

Prompt to improve affiliate marketing results:

"How can I optimize my affiliate marketing efforts on YouTube or TikTok to increase conversions? Suggest strategies like improving CTAs, adding more value to my affiliate recommendations, and testing different products."

- Example:
"Give me 3 ways to optimize my affiliate marketing strategy on YouTube. Focus on improving my CTAs, providing more value to my audience, and increasing affiliate link click-through rates."

With AI tools handling the editing, voice over, and monetization, you can focus on creating high-quality, consistent content while automating the processes that take time. From ad re venue to affiliate links, AI can boost your chances of growing and monetizing your YouTube or TikTok channel faster.

Online Courses or Mini Trainings

Creating anonline course can be overwhelming —but with the help of AI tools, you can streamline the entire process. From course brainstorming to creating slides, writing scripts, and even building email funnels for course sales, AI can assist in making your course creation process faster and more efficient.

STEP 1: BRAINSTORM COURSE IDEAS

AI can help you come up with course topics that are profitable and valuable to your target audience.

Prompt to brainstorm course ideas:
"Generate 10 profitable online course ideas for [audience] in the [niche] space. Focus on topics that are trending or evergreen."

- Example:
"Generate 10 profitable online course ideas for beginner entrepreneurs in the digital marketing niche. Focus on skills that are easy to teach and in high demand in 2025."

Prompt to identify course pain points:
"What are the 5 biggest challenges [audience] faces in [niche]? Generate a list of pain points that could be addressed in an online course."

- Example:

"What are the 5 biggest challenges small business owners face when it comes to growing their social media? Generate a list of problems that can be addressed with a course on social media marketing."

Prompt to validate course ideas:

"Which course topics in [niche] are most likely to sell well based on current trends and search volume in [year]?"

- Example:

"Which course topics in personal finance are most likely to sell well in 2025? Consider search trends for financial literacy and passive income."

STEP 2: BUILD COURSE SLIDES

Once you have your course ideas, AI can help you build your course slides by suggesting key points, headings, and visuals.

Prompt to outline course slides:

"Create an outline for a 10-s lide presentation on [your topic]. Include key points for each slide and recommended visuals."

- Example:

"Create an outline for a 10-slide p resentation on 'Building Your Personal Brand in 2025'. Include key points like 'Identifying Your Niche', 'Building an Online Presence', and 'Engaging with Your Audience'. Suggest visuals such as social media icons or branding examples."

Prompt for a slide script:
"Write a detailed script for the first slide in my presentation on [topic]. The slide is about [???]. Keep it informative and engaging."

- Example:
"Write a script for the first slide in my presentation on 'Building Your Personal Brand'. The slide should focus on defining your brand's purpose and how it impacts your business goals."

Prompt to suggest slides layout and design ideas:
"Suggest a layout and design for a course on [topic]. Include text, images, and graphics that would work well for a professional yet approachable look."

- Example:
"Suggest a layout for my course on 'Time Management for Entrepreneurs'. Include sections like 'Daily Prioritization', Time blocking', and 'Dealing with Distractions'. Suggest colors, fonts, and icons for a professional yet approachable feel."

STEP 3: WRITE COURSE SCRIPTS

Writing scripts for y our online course can be time-consuming, but AI can help you write detailed, engaging scripts that resonate with your audience.

Prompt to write a script for a course module:
"Write a script for a 5-minute video on [topic]. The tone should be motivational and easy to understand for new entrepreneurs."

- Example:
"Write a script for a 5-minute video on 'How to Set Achievable Business Goals'. The video will be part of a course for new entrepreneurs on goal-setting and productivity."

Prompt to create detailed lesson content for a course:
"Write detailed lesson content for a module on [topic]. Include actionable steps, examples, and tips for beginners."

- Example:
"Write detailed lesson content for a module on 'Building an Email List for Online Entrepreneurs'. Include step-by-step instructions, examples, and beginner-friendly tips for collecting emails and creating lead magnets."

STEP 4: EMAIL FUNNEL FOR PROMOTION

An email funnel is essential for promoting your course and driving conversions. Chat GPT can help you write a series of emails to warm up your lead s, promote your course, and encourage sign-ups.

Prompt to create an email sequence:
"Write a 5-day email funnel for promoting a course on [topic]. Day 1 should be an introduction, Day 2 should address a common problem, and Day 5 should be a strong call to action."

- Example:

"Write a 5-day email funnel for promoting my course on 'How to Build a Personal Brand'. Day 1 should introduce me and my story, Day 2 should address a common challenge of consistency. Day 3 should highlight testimonials, Day 4 should offer a special bonus, and Day 5 should be a final call to action to purchase."

Prompt for crafting a promotional email for course launch:

"Write a promotional email to launch my online course on [topic]. Focus on the benefits, key takeaways, and include a time-sensitive offer."

- Example:

"Write a promotional email to announce the launch of my new course on 'How to Create a Passive Income Stream in 2025'. Emphasize the benefits, key takeaways, and a special discount that expires in 48 hours.

Prompt for writing a post-purchase email sequence:

"Write a 3-part email sequence for new course buyers. The first email should welcome them, the second should provide a bonus resource, and the third should ask for feedback and reviews."

- Example:

"Write a 3-part email sequence for my new course on 'How to Make Money Online'. The first email should thank the buyer and introduce the course structure, the second should offer a free workbook as a bonus, and the third should ask for feedback and encourage leaving a review on the course platform."

Prompt to suggest affilia te programs for your course:
"Recommend affiliate programs I can use to monetize my course on 'Building a Personal Brand'. Suggest programs related to online marketing, social media tools, and course platforms."

- Example:
"Recommend affiliate programs for my course on 'Building a Personal Brand'. Suggest platforms that help with email marketing, social media growth, and personal branding tools."

Prompt to help optimize course pricing:
"Based on industry trends and competitor pricing, recommend a pricing strategy for my online course on [topic]. Should I use tiered pricing, early-bird discounts, or membership models?"

- Example:
"Recommend a pricing strategy for my online course on 'Starting a Successful Side Hustle in 2025'. Should I use tiered pricing, limited-time offers, or a payment plan?"

SELL YOUR COURSES AND MINI TRAININGS

Selling onlinecourses and mini-trainings can become fully automated, allowing you to focus on creating more value while AI handles the rest. Here's how you can use AI tools to drive traffic, create marketing content, set up sales funnels, and even engage with potential students.

STEP 1: AUTOMATE THE SALES FUNNEL

A sales funnel helps guide potential students from awareness to purchase. AI tools can assist you in creating the content and automation that will convert leads into buyers.

Prompt for creating a lead magnet funnel:
"Create a 5-email sequence for a course on [topic]. The first email should offer a free downloadable checklist, the second should introduce the course, and the third should include testimonials. Write en gaging copy and include a strong call to action in each email."

- Example:
"Create a 5-day email sequence for a free lead magnet. The lead magnet is a 7-day goal-s etting guide for aspiring entrepreneurs. The emails should promote a course on 'Building a Profitable Online Business'."

Prompt for creating a webinar funnel:
"Write a landing page copy and email sequence to promote a live webinar for my course on [topic]. The landing page should focus on the benefits of the course, and the email sequence sh ould remind attendees of the webinar date and provide a link to register."

- Example:
"Write a landing page copy for a 60-minute webinar on 'How to Make Money from Home in 2025'. Include a CTA to sign up for the free webinar and a reminder to attend."

STEP 2: GENERATE MARKETING CONTENT FOR SOCIAL MEDIA

AI can help you create engaging captions, posts, and video scripts for your Instagram, TikTok, and YouTube accounts to drive traffic to your courses.

Prompt for social media marketing campaign:
"Generate 5 Instagram post captions for a course on [topic] Focus on pain points like t ime scarcity and financial freedom, and include hashtags and CTAs."

- Example:
"Generate 5 TikTok post ideas to promote my 'Digital Product Creation' course. Each p ost should have a catchy hook, a benefit-driven message, and a CTA to visit my link in bio for more information."

Prompt to create video scripts for promotion:
"Write a script for a 60-second TikTok video on [topic]. Make it fun, motivating, and end with a CTA to visit my website for my free course preview."

- Example:

"Write a script for a YouTube ad promoting my course on 'Building Financial Freedom Through Real Estate'. The video should include an attention-grabbing hook, key benefits, and a limited-time offer for early-bird pricing."

STEP 3: CREATE COURSE SALES PAGES & OPTIMIZED PRODUCT DESCRIPTIONS

Your sales page is where the magic happens. Chat GPT can help you craft persuasive, high-converting sales copy and product descriptions that compel visitors to buy.

Prompt for writing a course sales page copy:
"Write a persuasive sales page copy for my online course on [topic]. Focus on the transformation it offers, include testimonials, and suggest pricing tiers (beginner, advanced)."

- Example:

"Write a high-converting sales page for my course 'Passive Income for Beginners'. Highlight the benefits of automating income streams and include a money-back guarantee and a CTA for sign-ups."

Prompt for writing an affiliate product description:
"Write a compelling product description for my affiliate link to an email marketing tool. Focus on the benefits, ease of use, and why it's essential for course creators to use it."

- Example:
"Write a product description for my affiliate link to a course platform. Mention the features like customizable branding, built-in sales pages, and automated student management."

STEP 4: SET UP ADS FOR YOUR COURSES

AI can also help you create high-performing ads to target potential customers across platforms like Facebook, Instagram, and YouTube.

Prompt for creating Facebook ads copy:
"Write an ad copy for a Facebook campaign promoting my course on [topic]. Make it attention-grabbing, benefit-oriented, and include a CTA to visit the landing page."

- Example:
"Write an engaging Facebook ad copy for my 'Content Creation for Beginners' course. Include social proof and a CTA to sign up for a free mini-cou rse preview."

Prompt for creating Google Ads copy:
"Write a Google Ads copy for my course on [topic]. Focus on the key benefits and use action-oriented language."

- Example:
"Write a Google ad for my course on 'Launching a Profitable Online Course in 2025'. Focus on high ROI and include keywords like 'course creation', 'passive income'."

STEP 5: Automate Sales & Engagement with Email Funnels

AI can help you set up and optimize your email funnels for promoting and selling your courses automatically.

Prompt for creating a course launch email sequence:
"Write a 7-day email launch sequence for my course on [topic]. Each email should build excitement, include a testimonial, and offer a time-limited discount."

- Example:

"Write a 7-day email sequence for the launch of my course on 'How to Write and Self-Publish Your First Book'. The emails should gradually reveal course benefits, and Day 7 should include a strong call-to-action with a special offer."

Prompt for a post-purchase email sequence:
"Write a 3-part email sequence for buyers of my course 'Mastering Facebook Ads for Be ginners'. The first email should thank them and provide access, the second should offer a bonus resource, and the third should encourage them to leave a review."

- Example:

"Write a 3-part email sequence for my course 'Create Your Own Online Store in 30 Days'. The emails should include immediate access instructions, a bonus checklist, and a request for a feedback survey."

BONUS: Use AI for Affiliate Marketing in Your Course Sales Funnel

Integrate affiliate marketing into your course sales funnel to earn extra passive income by recommending tools and services to your audience.

Prompt to find affiliate programs for your course:

"Suggest affiliate programs related to online business and course creation that I can recommend to my students as valuable resources. Include programs for tools like email marketing, website builders, or automation tools."

- Example:

"Find the best affiliate programs for online course creators in 2025. Recommend programs for tools that help with creating content, managing students, and automating marketing."

Prompt for add ing affiliate links to emails:

"Write an email to my students recommending a time management tool as an affiliate. The email should explain how the tool will help them stay organized while building their online business."

- Example:
"Write an email recommending an affiliate link to an AI-based video editing tool for my course students. Explain how the tool can save themtime while creating content."

Once your sales funnel is set up, and your AI-generated content is ready to go, you can automate the entire process — from course creation to ads, email funnels, and affiliate marketing.

By leveraging AI at every step, you'll not only save time but also boost your chances of success, allowing your course to sell itself.

Real-Estate Deal Autom ation

Using AI to automatetasks in realestate, such asfinding profitable deals, analyzing the numbers, and automating emails for deal follow-ups or marketing, can save you countless hours and boost your profits. Here's how to use Chat GPT and other AI tools to integrate these processes and streamline your real estate workflow.

STEP 1: FIND REAL ESTATE DEALS AI-powered tools like scrapers, lead generation bots, and

Zillow or Realtor APIs can help you find real estate deals based on specific filters like location, price, and property condition.

Prompt for finding properties on Zillow (via API or scraper):

"Scrape Zillow listings for dist ressed properties in [city or ZIP code]. Filter by properties that have been on the market for more than [X] days and are priced under $[X]. Include property type (single-family, duplex, etc.), price, and contact details."

- Example:

"Scrape Zillow listings for distressed properties in Detroit, MI. Filter by properties that have been on the market for more than 30 days and are priced under $50,000. Include property type, price, and contact details."

Prompt for using AI to find deals in a specific market:
"Find off-market properties for sale in [city or ZIP code] with high potential for fix-and-flip. Look for homes that have been on the market for more than 90 days and have been reduced by at least 10% from the original listing price."

- Example:
"Find off-market properties in Canton, OH, with a price reduction of at least 10% from the original listing price, and that have been on the market for more than 90 days."

STEP 2: INTEGRATE AND AUTOMATE DEAL ANALYSIS IN A GOOGLE SPREADSHEET

Automating your real estate deal analysis is key to quickly evaluating properties without spending hours on each one. AI can send the scraped data directly to a Google Spreadsheet where you can calculate ARV (After Repair Value), rehab costs, and profit margins.

Prompt to integrate with Google Sheets:

"Once I scrape Zillow listings for real estate deals, send the data to a Google Sheets file. The file should include columns for: Property Addres s, Price, ARV, Rehab Costs, Estimated Profit, and Purchase Date."

- Example:
"Once I scrape Zillow listings for properties in Detroit, MI, send the data to a Google Sheets file. Include the following columns: Address, L ist Price, ARV, Rehab Estimate, Profit Estimate, and Days on Market."

Prompt for creating a formula to calculate deal profitability:

"In Google Sheets, create a formula that calculates the profit margin for a real estate deal. Use the formula: Profit = ARV - (Purchase Price + Rehab Costs + Closing Costs). Highlight profitable deals where the profit margin is over $[X]."

- Example:

"Create a formula in Google Sheets that calculates profit margin for each deal. Use ARV, purchase price, rehab costs, and closing costs. Highlight profitable deals where the profit margin exceeds $10,000."

STEP 3: AUTOMATE EMAIL FOLLOW-UPS AND NOTIFICATIONS

Once you have scraped and analyzed the real estate deals,

AI can also automate email follow-ups, notifications, and marketing emails to either the seller or potential investors.

Prompt to automate email notifications for new deals:

"Create an email template that automatically notifies investors when a new profitable real estate deal is found. Include the property details, purchase price, ARV, rehab estimate, and estimated profit. Automatically send the email when a new profitable deal is entered into Google Sheets."

- Example:

"Create an email template that automatically sends out to my list of investors when a new profitable deal is added to Google Sheets. Include prope rty address, price, ARV, rehab costs, and expected profit margin."

Prompt for generating a follow-up email after initial contact with sellers:
"Write a follow-up email template to a property seller after an initial inquiry. The email should politely ask for more information about the property and offer to schedule a viewing."

- Example:
"Write a follow-up email to a seller of a distressed property. Ask for more details about the property and suggest scheduling a viewing. Include a polite and professional tone."

Prompt for automating email outreach using a CRM system:

"How can I automate email outreach to potential sellers using a CRM? Set up emails that trigger when new properties are added based on specific filters like price and location."

- Example:
"How can I set up automated email sequences using a CRM system to reach out to potential sellers of distressed properties in Georgia? Trigger emails when new properties meet certain criteria such as being priced under $60,000 and located in the 39901 ZIP code."

STEP 4: STREAMLINE THE DEAL CLOSING PROCESS

Once you've identified th e best deals, AI can help you track and organize your deal closing process, and even draft necessary documents like contracts or agreements.

Prompt for creating a closing checklist for real estate deals:
"Generate a real estate closing checklist for investors. Include steps like property inspection, due diligence, contract signing, closing costs, and funding."

- Example

"Generate a real estate closing checklist for my fix-and- flip business. Include steps like inspections, financing, title searches, and final walk throughs before closing."

Prompt for automating contract drafting using AI:
"Create a standard real esta te purchase contract template for a fix-and-flip deal. Include terms for inspection periods, contingencies, rehab costs, and closing dates. Automate this contract creation based on the property details I input into a Google Sheet."

- Example:

"Create an automated real estate purchase contract template that generates based on property details entered into my Google Sheets. Include sections on inspection period, purchase price, rehab cost estimates, and closing dates."

TIP FOR AUTOMATING YOUR REAL ESTATE DEALS

By using AI to find deals, analyze profitability, and automate follow-ups, you can save hours of manual work and focus more on closing deals and growing your portfolio. Tools like Google Sh eets, Zapier, CRM software, and email marketing automation help integrate AI into your business operations smoothly.

SUGGESTED TOOLS TO USE (FREE & PAID)

AI Writing, Prompting, & Content Creation

	Free	Paid
Chat GPT (Open AI)	☑	☑
Claude (Anthropic)	☑	☒
Copy.ai	☑	☑
Jasper	☒	☑
Writesonic	☑	☑

DESIGN TOOLS

	Free	Paid
Canva	☑	☑
Visme	☑	☑
Adobe Express	☑	☑
Creative Fabrica	☑	☑
BookBolt	☒	☑

VOICEOVERS AND VIDEO TOOLS

	Free	Paid
• Descript	☑	☑
• Murf.ai	☒	☑
• Pictory	☑	☑
• CapCut	☑	☑
• Runway ML	☑	☑

PRODUCT SELLING PLATFORMS

	Free	Paid
• Gumroad	☑	☑
• Payhip	☑	☑
• Etsy	☑	☑
• Amazon KDP	☑	☑
• Selfy	☒	☑

MARKETING & AUTOMATION TOOLS

	Free	Paid
MaierLite	☑	☑
ConvertKit	☑	☑
Zapier	☑	☑
Beacon	☑	☑
Metricool	☑	☑

SEO, RESEARCH & PRODUCT OPTIMIZATION

	Free	Paid
Google Trends	☑	☒
Ubersuggest	☑	☑
EverBee (for Etsy)	☑	☑
BookBeam	☒	☑
Publisher Rocket	☒	☑

REAL ESTATE AUTOMATION TOOLS

	Free	Paid
• Apify Zillow Scraper	☑	☑
• Google Sheets	☑	☒
• Zapier	☑	☑
• MailLite/ConvertKit	☑	☑
• CRM tools (REsimpli, Zoho CRM)	☒	☑

REAL ESTATE AUTOMATION TOOLS

	Free	Paid
• Apify Zillow Scraper	☑	☑
• Google Sheets	☑	☒
• Zapier	☑	☑
• MailLite/ConvertKit	☑	☑
• CRM tools (REsimpli, Zoho CRM)	☒	☑